Contents

Words printed in **bold** are explained in the glossary.

The team

We work at an opticians' practice. This is a place that you can go to if you need your eyes tested or to buy new eye glasses. Our team is made up of many people who are specialised in eye care.

▲ We are the optical advisers.

▲ I am the optometry manager.

▲ We are the **optometrists**.

◀ Opticians can be found in shopping centres or high streets.

▲ We are the laboratory technicians.

▲ I am the **dispensing optician**.

The reception

When you first walk into an opticians, you will be greeted by an optical adviser at the reception. Optical advisers do many jobs, such as arrange **appointments** for people who want an eye test, deal with **customers** and phone calls.

▲ I have just booked Amber and Ben for an eye test.

◄ I am telling a customer that his new glasses are ready to be collected.

▲ I am taking payment from a customer who has just had an eye test.

▼ Some people come to look for new frames to buy.

Appointments

The optometry manager gets **patients** ready for their eye test. When an appointment as been made by the optical adviser over the phone, the optometry manager sends them a reminder card.

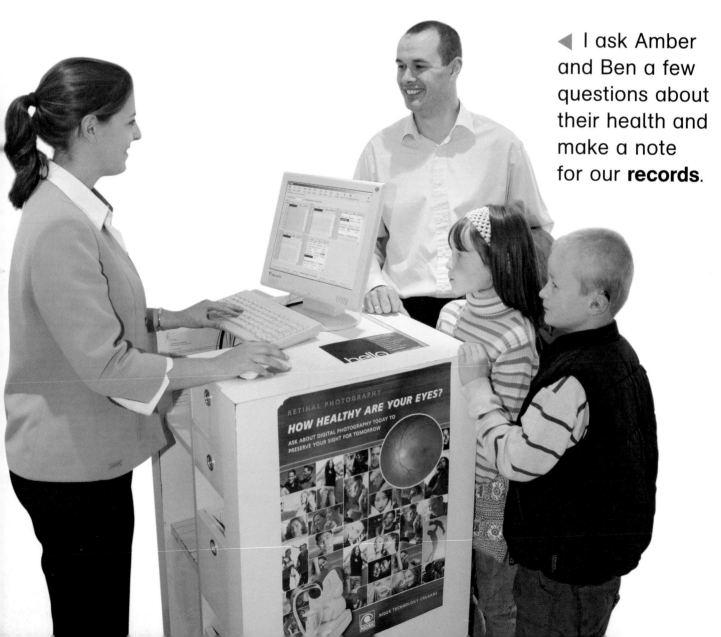

◀ I ask Amber and Ben a few questions about their health and make a note for our **records**.

New customers have to fill in a registration form. This records details about their **eyesight** and general health.

We have waiting area for customers to sit in while they wait for their appointment. ▼

Pre-examination

The optometry manager does some tests on the patient before they have an eye test.

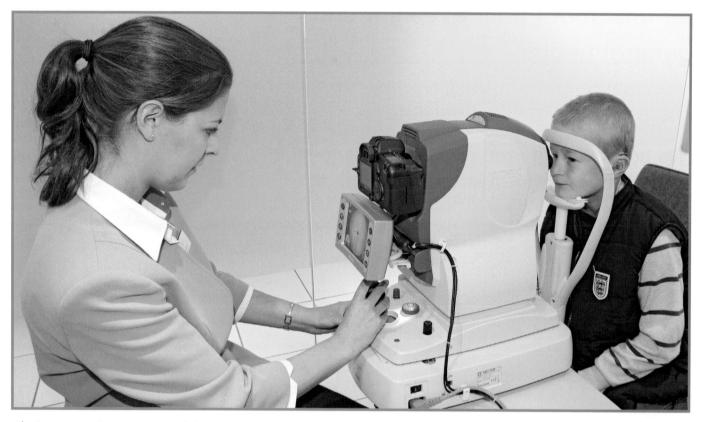

▲ I am photographing Ben's eyes with a special digital camera called a **Fundus Camera**.

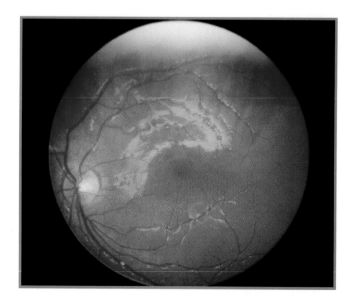

This camera takes a picture of the back of the eye. The more pink the eye is, the healthier it is. ▶

The optometry manager prints the results of the **pre-examination** test and gives this to the optometrist who will do the eye test.

I check Amber's eyes with an **autorefractor machine**. This measures how well the eyes adjust to focus on an object to create a clear image. ▼

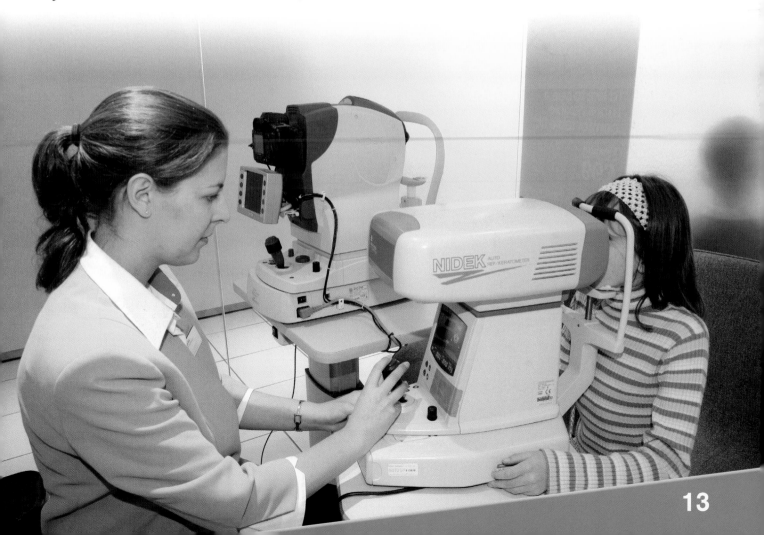

Eye test

Some people need glasses to see more clearly. Optometrists are trained to test our eyesight and **prescribe** glasses that help us see better.

First I check how well Ben can see. I cover each eye with an **occluder** and ask him to read the letters on a chart. ▼

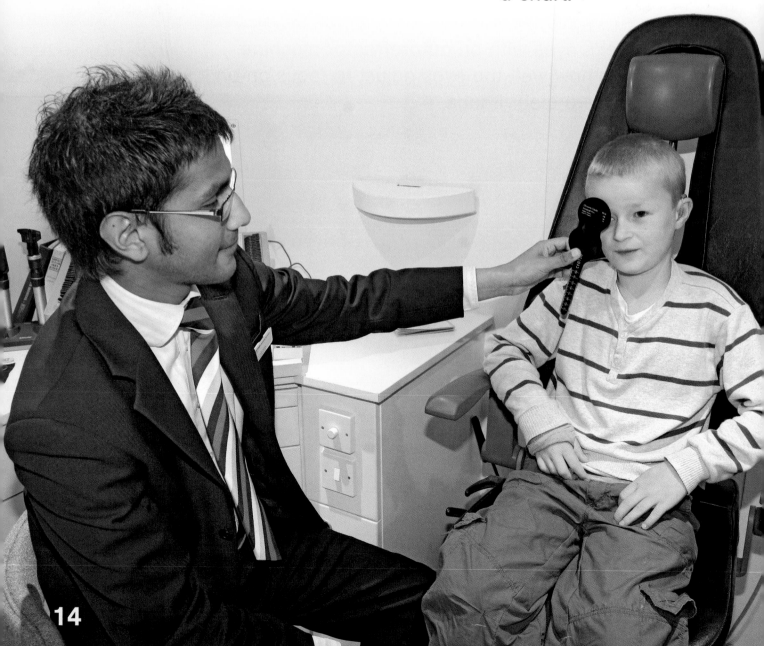

14

During an eye test, the optometrist looks right inside each eye to see how healthy the patient's eyes are. Eye **disease** can lead to eyesight problems.

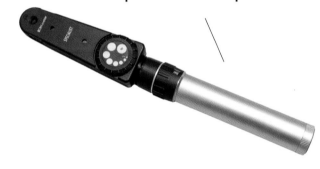

opthalmoscope

occluder

Next I look at the back of Ben's eyes using an **opthalmoscope**. ▶

Prescribing glasses

Optometrists use a special type of frame to measure the **prescription** of **lenses** a patient needs. Different strengths of glasses are needed depending on how good our eyesight is.

trial lenses

trial frames

I use **retinoscope** to see where light is being focused by the eye. Then I ask Ben to look through trial lenses to read some letters. ▼

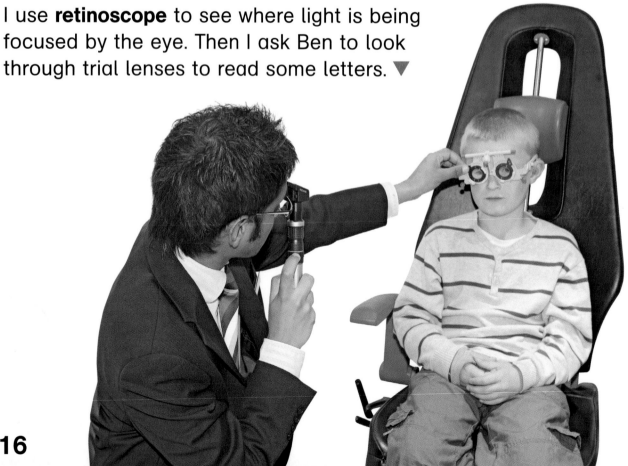

Everyone needs their eyes tested regularly, especially children whose eyesight can change as they grow up.

Five ways an optometrist can help us:

* Check our eyesight regularly.
* Prescribe glasses if we need them.
* Test to see if we are colour-blind.
* Protect your eyes from the sun with a hat or sunglasses.
* Check our eyes for other problems.

I slot different strengths of lenses into the trail frame until Ben can see the letters clearly. This measures the strength of the glasses he needs. ▼

Eye problems

Optometrists can examine our eyes for common conditions such as **squints** and colour-blindness. Fixation sticks are used to check if a patient has a squint. The optometrist tests to see if patient's eyes can look in the same direction at something, such as the picture on the stick.

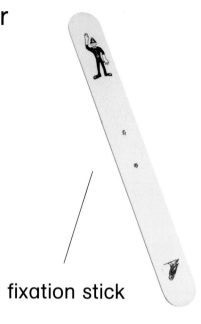

fixation stick

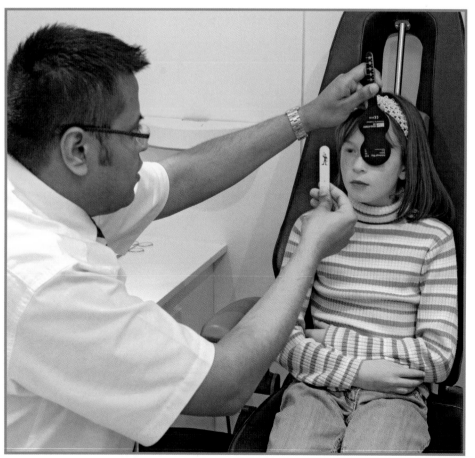

◀ I ask Amber to look at the stick as I move it towards her eyes.

People who are colour-blind cannot read coloured numbers against a coloured background, because they cannot see different colours.

Four facts about colour-blindness:

* People who are colour-blind find it hard to tell the difference between two colours:

* either red and green, or blue and yellow.

* One in twelve boys are colour-blind.

* One in two hundred girls are colour-blind.

Can you see the numbers here? ▶

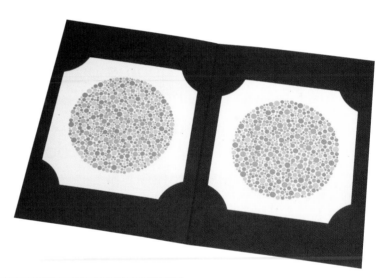

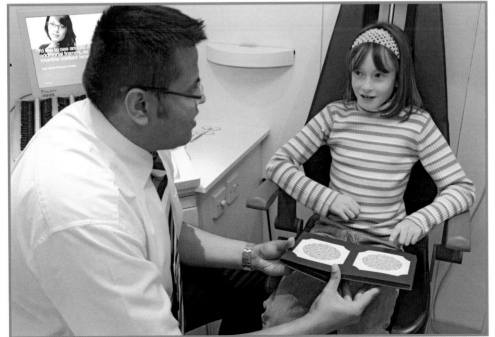

◀ Amber is able to recognise the numbers on each page.

Special equipment

Optometrists often use lots of machines. Each machine does a special job that helps the optometrist learn about our eyes. The patient does not feel anything.

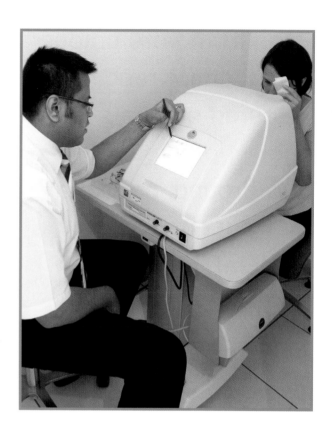

I am testing how good a patient's side vision is using a **Field Testing machine**. The patient has to cover one eye and say how many dots that she sees flashing. ▶

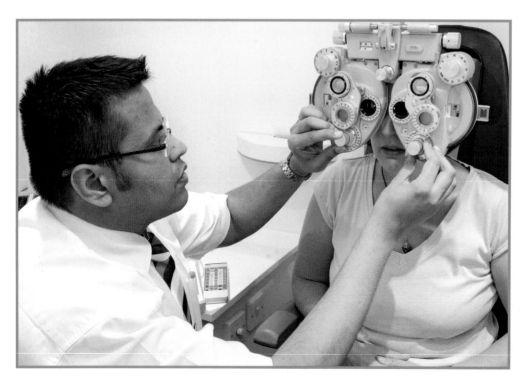

◀ I use the Phoroterhead to check if the patient is **long** or **short-sighted**. I adjust the lenses until the patient can see a letter clearly.

The **keratometer** measures the shape of the eyes. We use this to prescribe **contact lenses** for customers who wear them instead of glasses. ▶

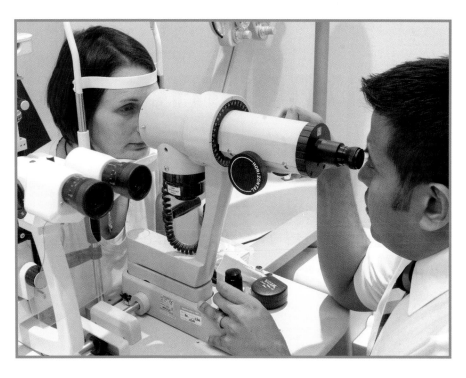

I use a **microscope** to look inside the eyes. A torch lights up the inside part of the eye. ▼

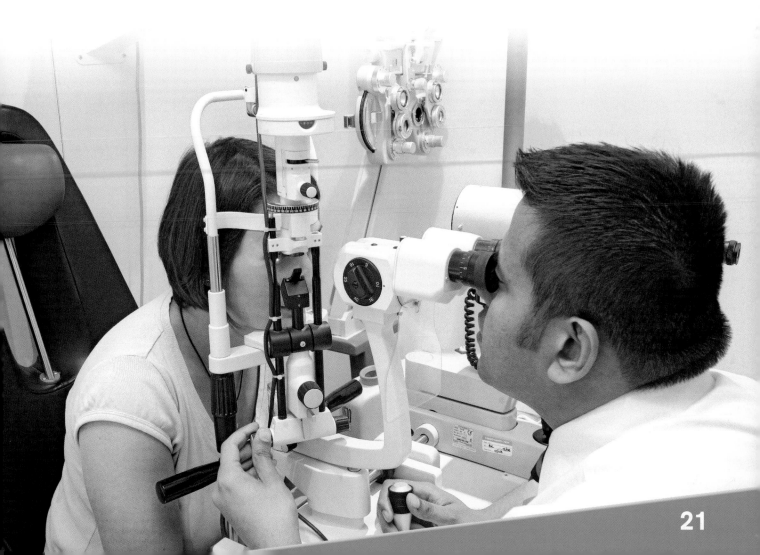

Dispensing opticians

After a patient has seen the optometrist, the dispensing optician helps them to find the right kind glasses they need.

I give Ben and Amber advice about what shape of glasses they should choose. ▶

I make sure that new glasses fit properly and do not slip off. ▼

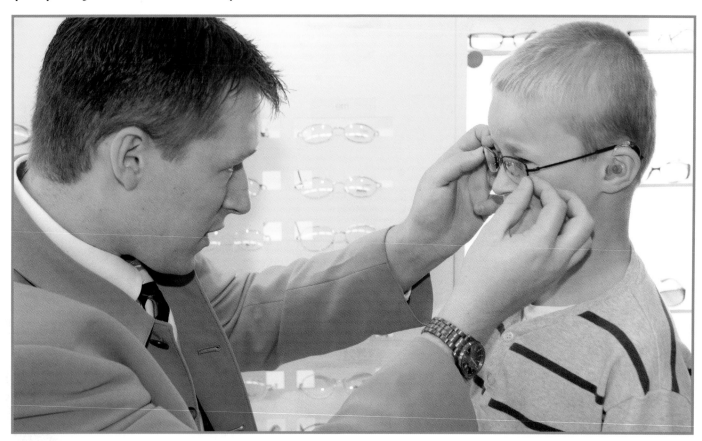

▲ Children have free eye tests. I help Amber and Ben's dad to fill out a special form for claiming back the money for their eye tests.

You might need glasses if:

* You can't read road signs.
* You get lots of headaches.
* You can't see the board in class.

Amber and Ben are very happy with their new glasses! ▶

Making lenses

New glasses are made in the laboratory at this opticians. It takes about an hour to make a pair of glasses.

We are laboratory technicians. We are trained to use lots of special machines to make glasses. ▶

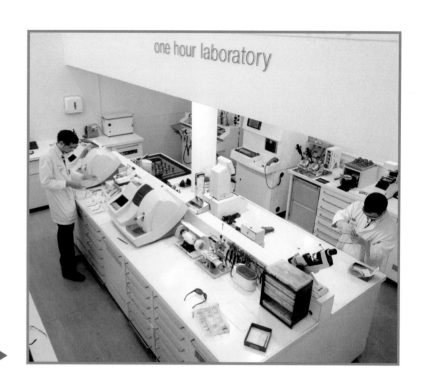

one hour laboratory

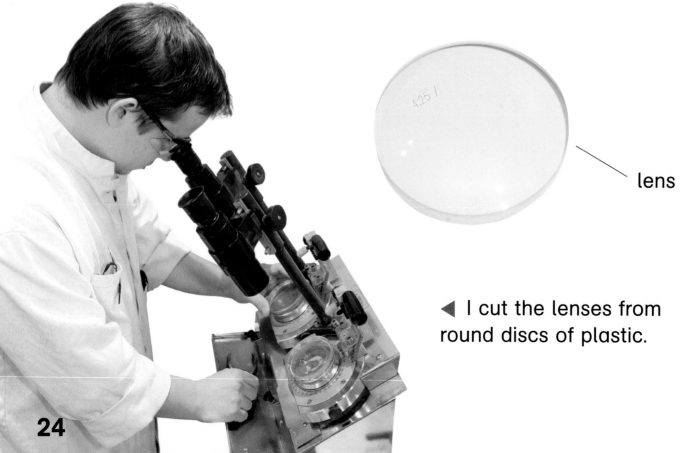

lens

◀ I cut the lenses from round discs of plastic.

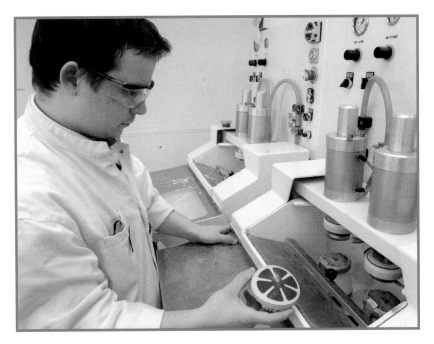

▲ Then, I polish the lenses to make them see-through.

This is called a lap and is used to polish lenses.

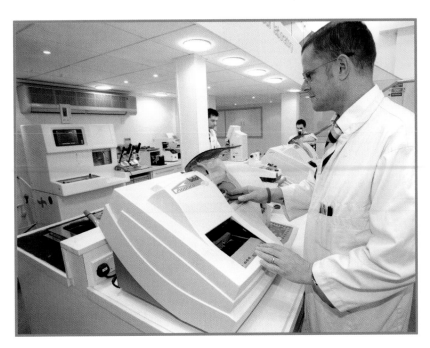

▲ Next, I use a machine to shape the lenses to fit the glasses frame.

Finally, the lenses are fitted into the frame. ▶

Buying new glasses

People can walk into an opticians and try on new glasses anytime. If you wear glasses, you need to make sure that new ones are comfortable.

Sometimes there are so many frames it can be difficult to choose a pair of glasses! ▼

Broken glasses can also be fixed at some opticians by the laboratory technician.

This is an optical screwdriver.
It tightens or loosens the tiny screws in glasses frames.

◀ I am replacing a shattered **lens** in this pair of glasses.

Glossary

appointment the time you have arranged to see the optometrist

autorefractor machine a machine to measure how well your eyes adjust to focus on an object

contact lenses tiny clear plastic lenses that sit on the surface of the eye to help a person see

customers someone who buys goods and services from a shop or business

dispensing optician an optician who is qualified to prescribe and give out glasses and contact lenses

eyesight a person's ability to see

field testing machine a machine that tests if a person can only see things straight in front of them

fundus camera a camera that takes a photograph of the back of the eye

keratometer the machine that measures the shape of the eyes so that the contact lenses fit well

lens the piece of clear plastic in a glasses frame that helps you to see

long-sighted someone who is long-sighted cannot see things that are very close

microscope an instrument that magnifies objects so they can be easily seen

opthalmoscope an instrument used by an optometrist to check the back of a patient's eye

optometrist someone who examines people's eyesight

patient a person who is looked after by an optician

pre-examination an assessment before a patient sees an optician

prescribe to advise on the best course of treatment

prescription a description of the strength of lenses

retinoscope an instrument used by an optometrist to see where light is being focused by the eye

short-sighted someone who is short-sighted cannot see things that are far away

squint when a person's eyes look in different directions

Quiz

Look back through the book to do this quiz.

1 What is a person who tests our eyes called?

2 How does an optometrist check if a patient has a squint?

3 What do laboratory technicians do?

4 Who can have free eye tests?

5 What does a keratometer measure?

6 What two colours can people who are colour-blind not tell the difference between?

Answers

1 optometrist

2 they ask the patient to look closely at a picture on the end of a small white stick to check if both eyes are looking in the same direction.

3 make and repair glasses

4 children, students and pensioners

5 the shape of an eye, so that contact lenses can be fitted properly.

6 red and green

Useful contacts

http://www.kidshealth.org/kid/body/eye_noSW.html
This website explains how the eye works, along with all the other parts of the body.

www.visionexpress.com/kids-zone/
Read up about the latest eye exam gadgets and gizmos, and discover how good your vision is by playing the interactive Super-vision game.

www.bootslearningstore.com/ks2/eyesight.swf
Insight into eyesight program that helps you find out how to look after your eyes and how problems can be corrected.

Come and visit us for an eye test soon!

Index

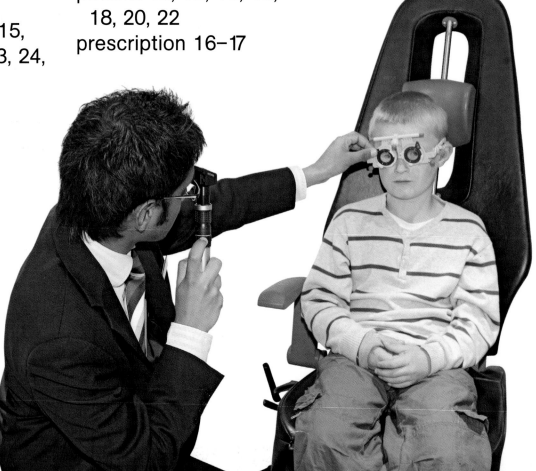